Intuitive Eating

A system that works to develop a positive relationship with food. Weight loss without dieting.

Scott Foblan

Table of Contents

Introduction

Diet, pills, surgery—the world has been going crazy for many decades now, in a continuous chase for the perfect body. Beauty standards may have changed over the past few decades. But in reality, our obsession with looking a certain way has not gone away. If anything, it has been growing at an exponential rate.

There is absolutely nothing wrong with wanting to look good. It helps your self-confidence, it allows you to feel good in your own skin, and it allows you to live healthily for longer.

When "looking good" becomes an obsession, though, and when the entire world seems to be swirling in circles around fad diets and plastic surgery like they're the new deities, there is something wrong going on.

If you have never dieted, and if you are looking for a clean, healthy, and sustainable way to lose extra pounds, you are in the right place. Intuitive eating, the main subject of the book at hand, is a concept that has been developed to go against the major trends and promote a view on health and healthy eating that restricts nothing and gives you complete freedom of choice.

If you have dieted before and have found yourself disappointed by all the false promises, you too are in the right place. Intuitive eating will "fix" everything wrong in every diet you have ever tried, precisely because it is not a "diet" in the real sense of the word, as much as it is a *lifestyle* choice.

This book is meant to help you understand why most diets out there fail miserably and why you should not even attempt to try them in the first place. On the surface, most fad diets promise near-miraculous weight loss systems that allow you to be happy, healthy, and beautiful.

However, these diets are rotten from their very core, precisely because they go against the very object of their "affection": the human body and the human mind, as well as the connection between them.

The sad truth about the diet industry is that it is all a business—and a very profitable one at that. To be more specific, the diet industry is worth no less than $72 billion (in 2018, and only in the United States) (Studies, n.d.). Regardless of whether you are looking at diet books, diet pills, or fitness programs that promise magic, they are all part of an industry that has been selling you lies, fallacies, and misconceptions.

"So why should we believe *you*, then," you might ask?

You shouldn't believe us because we say so, or because so many people have tried this system (and succeeded at it). You shouldn't even believe us because statistics show it (as you will learn in the chapters of this book).

You should believe us because intuitive eating is the only weight loss approach that makes true sense for pretty much everyone: experienced dieters and novices alike.

Intuitive eating is an approach that focuses on you and the relationship with your body—something no other fad diet truly promotes. Instead of eliminating food groups and falling into predetermined patterns that are bound to not work on *everyone*, intuitive eating focuses on allowing yourself to BE, allows yourself to ENJOY food, and allows yourself to NOT feel GUILTY.

Intuitive eating makes sense from a physiological and psychological perspective. Your body is perfectly engineered by Mother Nature to know what it needs—and our ancestors knew this all too well when they searched for food and when they decided to grow it in their own backyard. As such, no dietitian can ever tell *you* what to eat.

Yes, some of these fad diets may work on some people. But the vast majority of them fail (as statistics show it as well). And when you are yo-yoing from one diet to another, the only result you can see is not the weight loss you have been hoping for, but a weight *gain* and, most likely, an altered self-confidence.

It's time we all put an end to the craze. Not only is this whole cycle of weight loss and weight gain terribly unhealthy for your body, but it is incredibly unhealthy for your mind as well. Your self-confidence, your happiness, and your physical health are at stake here. Don't play with them!

There's no such thing as a perfect body, or even a perfect weight. There's no such thing as a perfect dietary plan. And, believe it or not, there's no such thing as "bad" foods either. Yes, you may have been told not to eat one thing or another, but if we have to be completely honest, weight loss, fitness, and health have nothing to do with complete restrictions. Instead, they have everything to do with learning how to balance out your diet both from a nutritional point of view and from a psychological one.

All there is your body and your relationship with it and with the food on your plate. Our book will focus on helping you reconnect with your body and rekindle your relationship with food, regardless of where you may be standing right now.

The first chapter of this book will help you understand the reasons that make diets fail so badly. We will present you with statistics and logical causes that make no less than 95% of the diets end up in the trash bin before they have even reached their goal.

The second chapter will focus on the main causes behind people's failures when it comes to dieting. We might be giving you a bit of a spoiler alert here, but the blame doesn't fall on the people who diet, as much as it falls on a system that is inherently broken.

Last, but not least, the third chapter of this book will focus on teaching you the main principles behind intuitive eating, why this is such a great solution, and why you should give it a try— regardless of whether you are a seasoned "dieter" or if you are "here" for the first time.

Overall, what we aim to do here is help you understand that food is not your enemy, and the only enemy you should have against extra pounds is your understanding of the entire "weight loss process."

We will debunk myths and crash stereotypes, and we will do it with logical arguments and statistics that show just how broken the whole concept of "dieting" is. More than anything, we will encourage you to truly reconnect with who you are so that you can better communicate with your body and its needs.

Weight loss should not feel like an endless, insurmountable mountain. It should not feel like pure torture. It should be all about being happier, not more miserable. And thankfully, there *are* techniques you can employ to make sure you don't lose your mind in the process of losing weight.

Thank you for choosing our book in your journey to weight loss! We truly hope you will find yourself happy at the end of it, but more than anything, we truly hope you will find your own "recipe" for happiness in relation to your eating habits.

Good luck and remember: loving yourself is the first and foremost important step towards happiness in every respect!

Chapter 1: Why Diets Fail

Research shows that 95% of all the dieting efforts fail. It sounds grim and hopeless, but there is a reason behind it all. Or, rather said, there is a *long list* of reasons that all these diets fail to provide their followers with the results they are looking for.

Moreover, even when you *do* make it to your weight goal, there's still a pretty high chance that you won't maintain the weight loss for more than 1–5 years—and, as you will see later on in this book, there are multiple reasons behind this as well (Weiss, n.d.).

The weight loss industry is booming—and it has been doing so for the last century or so. This is all the more worrisome as more than half of the 9-10 year old girls interviewed in a research study said they felt better about themselves when they dieted (Miller, 2015).

There is a crazy world of magic pills, fad diets, and miracle-making devices out there. From the moment you turn on your TV, PC, or smartphone, there's a pretty high chance you will bump into some kind of advertisement that promises weight loss. Depending on your browsing history and the kind of TV channels you are following, you might be more or less assaulted with weight loss "witchcraft." But sooner or later, you *will*.

The sad truth is that 99% of everything that is promised is a complete lie, or, at the very best, completely inadequate for you. We are all unique, amazing human beings and as such, we gain and lose weight differently. It's hard to fit everyone into a mold, and this is precisely why every single weight loss "miracle" that has been promised to you starts from a wrong premise.

On the other hand, there's a treasure trove of information on obesity, which seems to have tripled since the 1970s. Even more, as of 2016, nearly 40% of the world population is considered to be overweight. Out of these, 13% are also considered obese (WHO, 2020).

Extra pounds are not a matter of aesthetics only. If it were so, half of the people who are now struggling on a scale would just get larger clothing sizes and move along with their lives—because nobody should ever be defined by how many pounds they have.

Being overweight or obese is a matter of health, more than anything. It is a matter of the entire cardio-respiratory system malfunctioning to the point where people are passing away at younger ages than ever. It is an issue that makes hundreds of thousands live with diabetes in all its different forms. It is a problem that is literally not allowing your brain to receive the oxygen it needs.

Being overweight is a matter of physical and mental health—and, due to the large number of people affected by this condition, it is also a matter of public health. Billions of dollars are spent every year for the treatment of diseases and medical conditions associated with obesity. To be more specific, no less than $190 billion are spent every year on obesity-related illnesses (Economic Costs of Obesity, n.d.).

At the other end of the pole, eating disorders are tragically widespread as well. It is estimated that no less than 30 million people suffer from an eating disorder only in the United States (ANAD, n.d.). Anorexia and bulimia are just as dangerous as being overweight and, in the severe cases, they can be downright deadly.

It's clear that even in a world where access to information is more widespread than ever, we have an issue with our food. We eat too much or not enough, and we have been toned down into sedentary lifestyles that help with nothing at all.

Losing weight should not be about fitting into a smaller pair of jeans (although, let's face it, that's a pretty great motivator too). It shouldn't be about finding the love of your life. It shouldn't be about being one with the Joneses.

It should be about you. It's about who you are now, pushing your limits, being healthier, and allowing yourself to live your best life.

Yes, the vast majority of diets fail and a very few handful of those who are successful manage to actually maintain their weight loss for more than one year after reaching their target weight.

That doesn't mean things should stay as they are, or you comply with being overweight. It doesn't mean there is no way back.

This entire book will shift your perspective on weight loss, diets, and being *good* on yourself. And the chapter at hand is the foundation you need for your future self, as it will explain why everything you have tried (or wanted to try) so far is wrong.

We will tackle the subject of weight loss from the perspective of failure first and foremost, to help you understand *why* not many people make it to the finish line. We will move through statistics and research, through the psychology of weight loss, and, finally, we will list down the most important reasons "dieters" end up disappointed.

Let's get this ball rolling!

The Truth about Diets

Looking at statistics, the prospects of even attempting to lose weight can be quite dark. Why try if almost everyone else fails, and why would you even think you're special and that you can make it to your desired weight? Why not just comply and live as you are?

There are a lot of reasons this type of thinking is wrong, but we will discuss mindset a bit later on in the book. For now, we will just stick to: *stats are not there to show you that weight loss is impossible but to show that most people are doing it wrong.*

For example, it has been shown that more than one quarter of U.S adults are physically inactive, but that leaves 75% of the U.S adults who *are* physically active (Shahbandeh, 2019). You still don't see supermodels walking down the street on most days and the issue remains: more than one third of the people around the world are overweight, as shown in the previous section.

That means that, even with all the physical activity people engage in, they are still doing something wrong about their lifestyle because a pretty large proportion of those who are physically active might still fall into the "overweight" category as well.

Half of women are on a diet at any time (Dray, n.d.), but considering the large number of people who don't really meet their weight loss goals, it becomes clearer and clearer than we're living in an information bubble.

The truth about weight loss statistics doesn't show that we are incapable of losing weight (or losing weight correctly). It just shows that we have been bombarded with tons of poorly researched, biased, and even downright useless information. In the worst-case scenarios, the diet tips we're following are horribly dangerous—and even fatal.

We will debunk most of the diet myths in this book, as well as show you why everything you've been taught until now is wrong. We don't want to spoil it all, but here are some bits of information that will be revealed and expanded in this book:

- Carbs are not inherently evil (shocker, right?)
- No prescribed diet will ever make you lose weight in a sustainable way
- The vast majority of the weight loss pills are nothing more than glorified vitamin supplements
- Going to the gym is great, but not enough
- No fitness guru can ever tell you what to do or what to eat

Take any of the fad diets that have been going on for the past few decades and toss it into the trash bin—not because we say so, but because it is most likely based on a complete and utter lie. Take, for example:

- The Zone Diet is no magic way to portion your food. It's just common sense.
- The Keto Diet (together with pretty much all the low-carb diets out there) works just because it eliminates water from your body and because it eliminates an entire group of foods from your diet too. In consequence, you will lose a lot of weight in the first phase of the diet, and then somewhat sustain the weight loss because you will simply eat less, even from the things you *are* allowed to eat. In addition to all this, eating a diet focusing on fats (albeit the *healthy kind*) and protein is not balanced, and it can

cause health issues in its own turn (breaking news, but your body does need carbohydrates to).

- The Paleo Diet is just a "hipster" fad. No, our bodies don't "work" the same way our Paleolithic ancestors' did. We have evolved and we continue to evolve. For instance, did you know some people have stopped growing wisdom teeth because evolution deemed them unnecessary? (Krisch, 2016).
- The Blood Type Diet is complete gibberish. No, your blood type cannot affect what makes you lose weight and there's seriously no evidence to support the contrary (Watson, 2020).

If you rule out the vast majority of the diets out there, you will be left with two that are sensible enough to have a chance of being actually OK:

- Calories In, Calories Out
- The Clean Eating Diet

The main issue with these is that, similar to their siblings, they are unfeasible long-term. Counting calories can work, indeed, but for how long are you willing to do this? And even more than that, how do you make sure you won't fall into the other extreme and end up counting each and every single calorie you put in your body?

As for the Clean Eating Diet, it is probably the most sensible option (and, perhaps, the closest to what we will teach you in this book). The issues with it start to appear when you consider the fact that access to quality, clean food is scarce (and/or expensive). Furthermore, following this diet can also make you prone to falling into extremes, and you might just end up as the one person at your in-laws' 4th of July barbecue party who doesn't even touch the food.

How about weight loss pills? Do they help?

The short answer is "Yes, but…". Weight loss pills cannot magically burn the food you put in your body and they cannot wipe out a sweet tooth. They can do a lot when it comes to providing you with the vitamins your body needs (and which may sometimes be translated into cravings). But they cannot actually make you lose weight without any kind of effort on your end.

Statistics show that diet pills are not much better than a placebo pill—they can boost your weight loss efforts by 3% to 9% (Gunners, 2017), but that's pretty much *it*. With a bit more effort (and we really mean it when we say "a bit"), you can reach the same effects without the diet pills anyway.

Even more, although most weight loss pills are sold over the counter (or worse, over the internet!), the truth is that you shouldn't take them without consulting with your physician first. Even the simplest vitamins can do a lot of harm in certain circumstances, and weight loss pills can definitely fall in this category. Even more, whatever magic pill you have found on the internet and whatever "reviewers" might say about it, keep in mind that:

- It's most likely a scam.
- It can be *extremely* dangerous to buy any kind of medicine or supplement over the internet because you do not know for sure if they are regulated, and even if they are, you cannot know they are coming from an FDA-approved source.
- Most of the reviews you see are probably false and paid for by the company that's making the pills (it's seriously SO easy to hire 100 people and pay them $2 for a three-line review!)

- Even when they are recommended by bloggers or vloggers you follow, keep in mind that the company most likely pays them to say great things about their products.

Even for the pills that do work, there is a long list of reasons you shouldn't even touch them. They can be addictive, can cause toxicity in your body, be extremely expensive to take long-term (they can immediately stop their effect as soon as you stop taking them), and they can lead to anorexia and bulimia.

Diet pills are no joke, and they are most definitely not a good solution for anyone who tries to lose weight. Yes, there are cases when doctors might prescribe them, but those are the only cases when diet-adjutant pills are acceptable. Otherwise, our advice is to stay away from them as much as you can.

In addition to diet supplements, the weight loss industry is also crammed with all sorts of products that promise you the moon and the stars and a size four pair of jeans by summertime. To save yourself the time and the money, we will cut it short: no, they don't work.

Sauna belts, vibrating massage belts, body lotions, and all sorts of so-called miracle-makers - they are advertised everywhere you turn your head. Yes, they might help a teeny tiny bit, but they are even less efficient than diet pills. They might help by toning up your body a little, but there is no scientific background to ever be able to provide sufficient evidence that any of these products do more than add an extra burden on your credit card.

The absolute truth about weight loss can be summed up in three main ideas:

- Nobody can ever dictate what YOUR body likes or doesn't like best—and as such, any diet that tells you to only eat one thing or another relies on presumptions that have no real foundation in science.

- There's a high failure percentage among people who attempt dieting, but that's not because we're genetically incapable of losing weight. It is about doing it wrong.
- Weight loss products of all kinds (devices and pills alike) are inefficient, expensive, and potentially dangerous.

By this point, you might feel completely hopeless and disillusioned, which is completely understandable given that you have been bombarded with lies and misconceptions all your life.

The purpose of this entire section is not to show you that weight loss is impossible, as we have already mentioned it. The whole purpose of all of this is to help you open your eyes and understand that most of the things you have been told to do are quite wrong in essence, for a variety of reasons. Some are blatant lies, others are just make-believe, and others are downright dangerous.

You shouldn't feel like you just lost all hope. The whole point of this section was to lift the burden off your chest and help you see that you cannot walk the same wrong path that everyone else is. You do not have the time or the money to do that, and you do not want to risk your most precious asset in the process: your health.

The fact that most of the diet tips out there are inefficient and/or insincere should only mean one thing for you: there *is* something that works, and that "something" eliminates the issues other diets have.

We will discuss the specifics of this "something" later on in this book. For now, however, it is important for you to focus on understanding why you shouldn't make the same mistakes as 90% of the dieters out there.

The Psychology of Weight Loss

Even if you have the best trainer in the world, the most talented Clean Eating chef at your disposal and all the money in the galaxy to hire nutritionists, and a team of pros to help you look great and be healthy, they can do absolutely nothing for you if you do not understand how your mind functions.

Every single change starts with a thought. It has been so since the beginning of times, when Homo Sapiens thought it would be nice to have some tools to help them in their daily tasks.

It's still happening, in every single person who sets a goal, regardless of whether or not it is related to weight loss. The moment you say, "I want to...," you are already sending a certain energy out in the Universe. It may not be enough to actually make that wish come true, but it is a powerful message that will boomerang back to you and help you stick to your plan of action.

The psychology of weight loss is very tightly connected to that incipient thought—but, unlike what a lot of fitness gurus will tell you, it is a lot more than that. One cannot deny the power of setting your mind to a goal and actually following through with a plan. But, if we have to be honest, weight loss is a bit more complex than that, in most situations.

To understand the psychology of weight loss, you must first understand the psychology of weight gain. In reality, there are just three main causes that lead to weight gain:

- Health issues
- Overeating
- Insufficient exercise

Everything else that might cause weight gain is a byproduct of these causes. Let's take a look at each of them in more detail, one by one:

Health Issues

Certain health issues can cause weight gain, and this is a fact no medical body in the world will ever be able to deny. There are two main ways health issues can cause weight gain:

- **Directly:** This is in the case of hypothyroidism, for example.
- **Indirectly:** This is in the case of chronic pain (which prevents patients from moving) or certain mental health issues (such as depression, which can cause weight gain as well).

Health issues that influence one's weight in a direct way are quite rare. However, weight gain caused by health issues is often considered to be mild (Sanyal & Raychaudhuri, 2016) (but there are documented cases that show a more significant weight gain associated with these health issues).

Most times, when health issues are connected to weight loss, it is because of their indirect influence. People who suffer from chronic illnesses (such as fibromyalgia, for example), find themselves chained to a sedentary lifestyle they did not choose. Living with pain can make it very difficult to get the amount of physical exercise one needs to stay healthy and fit. Also, living with chronic pain can also make one more predisposed to emotional eating as well.

In most cases where health issues are linked to weight gain, it is of the utmost importance for the patient to seek treatment for their primary health problem before they even attempt to lose weight by traditional means. For instance, someone who suffers from fibromyalgia might get serious injuries if they force their bodies at the gym and they need a plan of action that is adapted to their needs.

The same goes for people who suffer from mental health issues as well. Depression has been long linked with both weight gain and weight loss, but before one even attempts to tackle the weight problem, they should seek therapy for their depression first. Of course, weight loss and therapy can happen concomitantly, but what is important to remember here is that weight loss, no matter how successful, cannot and should not replace therapy.

Overeating

In a world where rich countries throw away tons of food and under-developed countries are starving, it is hard to imagine how anyone could be overeating.

And yet, overeating is the most common cause for weight gain. What a lot of people don't understand is that it is extremely easy to overeat. Take, for example, the basic intake of someone who does office work. If that person is 5'5" and weighs 160 pounds, they should consume about 1,700 calories to maintain their weight.

That might seem like a lot of calories, but here's how it can all break down:

- One cup of coffee with milk and all the fancy extras can get as high as 300 calories or more.
- Two fried eggs, a slice of toast and two slices of bacon can get as high as 400 calories or more.
- One tuna salad sandwich can get as high as 500 calories.
- One frozen dinner can get as high as 500 calories.
- Two snacks (like a handful of nuts and an apple, or a fruity yogurt and a couple of crackers) can get as high as 200 calories.

A person who eats like this will be 200 calories over their daily needs. In less than three weeks, that would translate into an extra pound on the scales. Add a bit more calories to that breakfast and replace the tuna sandwich with a burger and you will see how easy it is to be seriously overeating on a daily basis.

Another issue not many people realize when it comes to overeating is that it can happen even when you eat clean, healthy foods. For example, avocados are great for your body— they are all about the good fats and they taste amazing on toast. But did you know one avocado can get as high as more than 300 calories?

In this paradigm, you can technically gain weight even if you eat nothing but kale leaves from morning until dawn. It would probably take several pounds of kale leaves to move past your necessary caloric intake, but it can *theoretically* be done.

This is not meant to scare you, nor is it meant to push you into a mad calorie-counting craze. This is just to show that overeating is really "easy" and that most people don't even realize it.

In addition to "regular" overeating, binge eating, and emotional eating can put a real toll on your weight maintenance efforts. One night of going to the fridge and wiping off all the cheese in it won't do much harm, in all honesty. But two, three, or forty-three nights of this kind of eating can really add up on the scales.

Binge eating and emotional eating are very tightly connected to each other, and they should be treated with utmost seriousness. There are very stringent causes that push people into this kind of behavior, and it is extremely important for you to be fully aware of these causes so that you eliminate them from your life.

Food is comforting and good, and when other areas of your life are not doing that great, it is very easy to turn to comfort food and overeat it. This stems from issues that are much deeper than any kind of nutritional knowledge you may not possess yet. It is important to deal with these issues when you proceed on a weight loss journey because it will allow you to stay on track and make sure that you do not replace one outlet with another (i.e. replace food with another comforting action or substance).

Binge eating can also be related to an improper meal balance throughout the day. Most nutritionists advise people to have at least three main meals throughout the day. Although this has been debated quite a lot, one thing is for certain: eating more meals makes it less likely for you to overeat. The reason this happens is because you are not starving yourself for a longer period of time, only to turn the fridge upside down as soon as you get in front of it.

We highly recommend you deal with your overeating or binge eating issue if there is one. Some of the most important tips to keep in mind include the following:

- **Forget about dieting in the traditional sense of the word.** We will discuss more about this in the next chapters (as this is precisely what the entire book is focused on).
- **Don't skip meals.** Whether or not you need three, five, eight, or two meals a day doesn't matter. Listen to your body, listen to your hunger cues, and allow yourself to fall into a meal pattern. When this happens, avoid skipping the meals in your own pattern of eating.
- **Be mindful.** It might seem like a very random tip but being mindful of your body helps you "listen" better. It helps you know when you are hungry and when you are eating for completely different reasons (boredom or emotional problems, for example). It also helps you be more careful about *what* exactly you are eating.
- **Get some fiber.** One of the main reasons low-carb diets are quite unhealthy is because they frequently limit the amount of fiber that gets in your body. Sure, you can get fiber from a lot of vegetables, but when low-carb diets fall into the *almost no carb* diet, it's hard to reach a fiber intake that is healthy for your body. Fiber helps with digestion, helps you feel fuller, and it helps you avoid overeating and binge eating as well.
- **Declutter your kitchen and your eating space.** No matter where you cook and eat, declutter the space around you. Clutter makes it difficult for your brain to fully process what is going on and as such, it makes it easier for you to overeat without even realizing it.
- **Avoid eating in front of the TV (or computer).** Your meal time should be about eating more than anything. When you sit in front of the TV and eat, you are far more likely to overeat precisely because you are not allowing your brain and your body to fully process the

fact that you are eating. As such, you will miss the moment when you are full as well, and you will be a lot more likely to eat more than you need.

- **Exercise.** We don't need to tell you this, but physical exercise is key for your health from every point of view. Regular exercising helps your mind and your body stay healthy. It also helps you be more mindful and careful about what you are eating (and how much), especially when you are fully aware of how much effort you have to put into burning bad foods. Keep in mind that exercising can also increase one's appetite, so you might want to keep that in check.

- **Get your breakfast.** There's a reason they call it the most important meal of the day. If you start your day on an empty stomach, you will be far more likely to overeat throughout the day. A healthy and nutritious breakfast will keep hunger at bay for a few hours and it will also provide you with plenty of energy to go about your day until your next meal.

- **Eat more protein.** Protein makes you feel full for longer. The key is making sure you are getting healthy proteins, from lean, low-cholesterol sources (such as chicken, fish, turkey, or egg whites, for example). You might not be able to follow this all the time, but the more mindful you are about what you put in your body, the more likely it is that you will succeed in the end.

- **Plan your meals in advance.** If your binge eating problems are connected to chaotic eating, it might help to plan your meals in advance. Take some time every Sunday to plan out your food for the week. There are a lot of meals you can prepare in advance so that you can stick to your plan and ensure that you do not fall off the wagon.

- **Sleep.** You might not realize this, but bad sleeping patterns have a tremendously negative effect on your eating patterns. Insufficient sleep slows down your metabolism, which makes it more likely for you to gain weight. Even more, it makes you more prone to be moody (and thus, more prone to binge eating as well, especially when this has been an underlying issue).
- **Keep a journal.** Start a journal where you jot down what you eat every day, at every meal. If you eat on an emotional basis, it might be great to include a mood pattern tracker in the same journal as well. This will help you become more aware of bad eating patterns connected to bad moments, and as such, it will make you less prone to binge eating and overeating.
- **Talk to someone.** It might not seem so when you feel like drowning in your own sorrow and sadness but talking to someone can ease your mind. Even more, it can help you see things through a different perspective. As mentioned before, if you have been haunted by depression, anxiety, or any other kind of mental health problems, it is extremely important for you to talk to a specialist as well. A friend can only lend you their ear and their soul—a therapist, on the other hand, can help you find your way back to mental wellness.

Overeating is a real concern and it should be addressed with all seriousness, regardless of whether or not it is connected to emotional issues. It is important for you to be honest with yourself and dig deeper into the reasons that push you into overeating. Once you have identified those, you can reverse-engineer the patterns that led you to this point and bring yourself back to a healthier relationship with food.

Insufficient Exercise

Judging by the statistics we have also presented earlier in this book, it is quite clear that we do not move enough. The American Heart Association recommends people to perform heart-pumping activity for at least two and a half hours per week (AHA, n.d.). This does not necessarily include slow walks by the riverside, but it doesn't limit the fitness activity to things you can only do in a gym either.

You might love dancing, roller-skating, jogging or you might just love a good round of Tae-Bo. Whatever it is, make sure you do it on a regular basis. If it makes your heart pump, it's great for you.

Exercising is not about weight loss only. It's about your mental and physical health. It helps your heart function, it helps you breathe better, it helps your digestion, and it helps your muscles and your bones. It also helps you to be happier, as endorphins are released after heavy exercise to help the body recover.

Exercising is essential. It is not enough to make you lose significant amounts of weight, but it is something you have to do for your own well-being. It might be difficult to pick it up, indeed. However, once it has become a regularity in your life, exercising can also be addictive in the positive sense of the word. The more you practice it, the more likely it is that you will never want to give it up. And there's absolutely nothing wrong about that!

OK, so this is how people gain weight. How do they *lose* it then?

If we had to simplify this to one sentence, it would be this: people lose weight by reversing the problems that led to weight gain in the first place. If it is a biological health issue, treating it will help you lose weight. If it is an emotional health issue, addressing it will help you lose weight.

The pattern to follow is simple on the surface and painfully intricate when you go in-depth. But if you want to make sure you succeed, you have to be realistic from the very beginning and accept that this whole weight loss "thing" cannot be done overnight. No matter the reason behind your weight gain, it will take time for you to shed those pounds and make sure you build a personalized system that allows you to *keep* them off as well.

The psychology of weight loss is based on reverse-engineering the habits that led you to weight gain. But more than anything, it is about being realistic, honest, and determined. Without these three ingredients, your weight loss journey will be inefficient, impossible to sustain in the long run, and probably quite unhealthy as well.

So, Why Do Most Diets Fail?

Most diets fail because a lot of people expect miracles—and, as such, the weight loss industry responds to these expectations by creating unrealistic "diets" and "dietary products" that promise everything. Instead, the vast majority of these diets and products end up delivering nothing much in return.

Just like in matters of love and dating, once you have been disappointed by dieting, it is extremely difficult to go back and try something new. Your body and your mind are working hard against your broken heart and, as such, you will inadvertently push yourself into a never-ending cycle of mild weight loss, weight gain, and disappointment.

It's easy to understand why this is completely unhealthy from so many points of view. On the one hand, it is unhealthy for your body (because it will keep on following the same yo-yo pattern). On the other hand, it is unhealthy for your mental state as well (because one can only face so many disappointments, in the end).

More than anything, diets fail because there's an entire mechanism meant to make you fail. The weight loss industry would die out a quick and painful death if someone came along and sold the ultimate pound-shredder. The more people would try it, the less people who need weight loss products would be out there on the market and as such, 99% of the diet products and fitness gurus would simply have to retire.

This is not a conspiracy theory, mind you. It is simply a mechanism of offer and demand, a mechanism upon which capitalist economies have been built, and a mechanism that is not inherently bad, but which can be easily manipulated into mentally and physically unhealthy patterns.

Diets fail because there is a mountain of misinformation out there, and people set up for unrealistic expectations, and, most of all, because everything you have been taught about dieting goes against every single one of your instincts.

Your body is perfectly engineered to know what it needs. An avalanche of ads, a stressful life, and a large number of low quality tips can stray you away from what your body truly needs. It can make you prone to binge eating on fast food products because you are sad. It can make you prone to anorexia and bulimia when you fall into these disorders. It can make you feel like you have to eat a certain way or completely avoid certain products because you've been told they're bad for you.

But the absolute truth is that no food out there is inherently *bad for you*. What you want is not to eliminate pizza from your life. What you really want is to make sure you find the right balance and only eat pizza when you are truly craving it or when you are celebrating something that matters to you.

Have you ever noticed how people who have everything seem to be terribly unhappy and unexcited with everything they have? When you are swimming in an abundance of objects and experiences others only dare to dream of, it becomes easy to be less appreciative of what you have (unless you make a conscious effort against this tendency).

The same goes with bad eating patterns as well. When you get pizza every other night, it stops being as delicious as it once was. Instead, it becomes a regular comfort you turn to because you had a bad day or because you just want something nice to go with your TV show.

Your body knows this. Your body knows when it is fed up with too much of one thing. If you stop from your cycle and listen, you will hear your body screaming at you. Because, as mentioned before, the human body is perfectly engineered. As such, it will *know* exactly what it needs and how much of it is needed.

We will discuss more about this later on in the book, but if we have to sum up this first chapter in just a few words, it would be this: most diets fail, and the reason they do is because "dieting" has been incorrectly preached about for more than a century now.

It's time to break the pattern and return to truly listening to your body—which is precisely what we will discuss further on in this book.

Chapter 2: Why People Haven't Been Successful So Far

We have already discussed the fact that the vast majority of diets are utterly unsuccessful. That is the bigger picture: the ways in which the weight loss industry has been maneuvering the truth to its own advantage.

That is what we have discussed in the first chapter of this book. Understanding the weight loss (and weight gain) context will help you better understand why *you* might have been unsuccessful with your diets so far.

The first chapter might have provided you with some information regarding this. You might have learned that you have been lied to by all the fad diets and weight loss supplements. Or you might have learned that there might be underlying emotional problems connected to your binge eating problem.

Whatever it is, you have most likely already scratched the surface of what made you gain weight and prevented you from losing it until now.

This chapter will help you go even more in-depth on these issues. We will tackle your relationship with eating, what the media is selling you as a "weight loss miracle," and what are some of the worst mistakes you can make throughout your weight loss journey. You might be familiar with some of the tips we will share in this chapter but try to look at them through the lens of everything that has been discussed until now—

particularly, the fact that you should be listening to your body instead of anyone else.

Let's start digging!

Your Relationship with Eating

The wonderful thing about being a human being is that we are beautifully complex and unique. On the surface, we're all the same. Science has even narrowed us down to a pyramid of needs (McLeod, 2018) that is universally accurate when it comes to what people need to be happy and thriving.

In-depth, we are so shockingly different that it makes it nearly impossible to find two people who will have the same life story and react the same way to the same situations. Twins who grew up in a healthy environment can be an example here. Although they are structurally very much alike and they received the same type of education, each of them will have his or her own personality, sets of interests, and unique emotional shades. Even Siamese twins follow in the same pattern, and those who were graced with the gift of growing up into their adulthood can definitely attest to the fact that, although barely separated, they are very different in essence.

Your relationship with eating is most likely not the same as your neighbor's relationship with eating, and it is most likely not the same as your mother's either. Just like in a love relationship, you bring in your own history, your own emotions, and your own personality. If you want to put it in a more humorous way, no two people will look at a slice of pizza the same way -

precisely because the same slice of pizza can evoke different memories, different centers of the brain, and different new thoughts as well.

To understand why your weight loss efforts have not been as successful as they should have been, it is important to first make sure that you understand where you stand in your relationship with eating in general.

To do that, we want you to take a sheet of paper and write down your answers for the following questions, in as much detail as you possibly can. Don't mind the "artistry" of the writing itself, just allow your pen to flow on the paper. Keep in mind: you have to be terribly honest with all of this. Also, we recommend you keep these answers and look at them every now and again throughout your weight loss process.

1. Why do you eat? Do you only eat when you are hungry?
2. If not, what are some other reasons that make you eat?
3. Which times of the day do you eat most? Why?
4. What is your favorite food? Why?
5. Do you associate your favorite food with happy memories?
6. Do you feel like you eat too much, or too much of the "bad" foods?
7. How much is really "too much?" Have you ever measured your caloric intake, just for a "test run" to see how much you are really overeating (or undereating)?
8. Do you ever feel guilty after eating?
9. Do you ever perceive food as a reward or as a punishment for something you did?
10. Have you ever had this relationship with food, or is there something in your past that triggered it or led to its formation?

Be extremely honest with your answer and write as much as you can. Take your time, don't rush, and avoid any kind of interruption. By the end of this exercise, you should have figured out where you lie in your relationship with food and as such, you will understand what main mistakes you have been making so far.

Nobody can *tell* you what issues you have in your relationship with food and eating. YOU are the only one who can figure this out by being blunt and painfully honest with yourself.

The low-carb diet will tell you the main problem you have is eating too many carbohydrates. The Paleo diet will tell you the main problem you have is that you don't understand evolutionary changes in your body. Diet pills will tell you the main problem you have is related to some sort of vitamin or mineral deficiency.

But the truth is that most people don't fall in these categories (or at least they don't fall into *just* one of these categories). The absolute truth about weight loss promises is that nobody can promise you a ready-made plan, just like clothing manufacturers cannot actually promise their "one size fits all" items will look the same on everyone (or that they will even fit everyone).

It is up to you to determine where you lie in your relationship with food. This is the first and foremost important step towards being *better*, not just from a weight-related point of view, but from an overall point of view.

The Media vs. Weight Loss

To get this straight from the very beginning: we are not blaming the media (or the weight loss industry) for the high percentage of failure in weight loss programs. We are not blaming the actual participants in all of this either.

If we have to be honest, it's a mixture of everything: unrealistic expectations are set from both the ends of those who try to lose weight and from the end of those who sell weight loss products, diets, and plans.

The media is a massive participant in the entire issue, mostly because it has been selling illusions of perfection for decades in a row. From ads showing happy families in the 1950s to Instagram models these days, mainstream media has been following the same toxic pattern of setting the bar unrealistically high and then helping companies sell products that are unrealistically promising.

What you have to know is that movie stars, ads, and Instagram celebrities are not real. They are just tapping into a human need: that of perfection. Yes, a lot of women and a lot of men look absolutely astounding and yes, you can get there too. But you can't do it just like that; you have to accept the fact that, most of the time, it is in these people's job descriptions to look unworldly beautiful.

This also means there is an entire team of people behind them to make sure they look spotless. They have nutritionists and fitness trainers, surgeons and fashion designers, hairstylists and makeup artists, photographers and graphic editors that are all working to make celebrities and people in ads look surreally appealing.

You have to understand that although you can definitely aim for the same level of fitness and good looks, you also have to know that:

- It will take time, and even more so because you do not have an army of people following what you eat and how you move every step of the way.
- Even in the case of the most attractive people on Earth, there are still a lot of "tricks" applied both before and after the picture or the movie is shot.

Being aware of what your realistic goals should be is extremely important regardless of what dietary plan you might choose to follow. When you set your goals too high, you are basically working against your body, against your nature, against everything that feels "in its place" about you and your life. You also generate unnecessary stress and put a lot of pressure on your mental and physical health (which can spiral out of control really easily).

There is absolutely nothing wrong with looking up to celebrities, but it would be terribly wrong of you to expect to look exactly like them. Unless you have an entire team of people working to make your appearance flawless, you need to understand that there is no point in pressuring yourself out of the healthy limits to achieve some sort of "dream body."

Aside from consistently presenting us with unrealistically good-looking people, the media is also poisoning your mind with a lot of information meant to do nothing more and nothing less than *sell* you weight loss products.

Nobody says that having a static bike in your house won't help, or that you might not benefit from a green tea, but, just like in the case of looking up to celebrities, it is of the utmost importance to make sure you set your expectations correctly.

The media is full of lies, and not just when it comes to weight loss. You shouldn't necessarily stop watching movies or reading about your favorite celebrities, but you should definitely take everything with a grain of salt.

In addition to all this, the media is constantly making us feel inappropriate. Even with all the healthy foods in the world and all the working out, there's still a pretty big chance you will never look like your favorite stars, and that is, again, because a team of professionals helps them. This doesn't mean you shouldn't aim for better, but it does mean that you should listen to your body and your inner self when you have reached your goal weight and goal fitness level.

Remember, weight loss is not about fitting into a better pair of jeans or looking like Scarlett Johansson. It is about feeling great in your own skin, both from a physical point of view and from a mental one. If you allow the media to feed you blatant illusions, you will never feel truly satisfied and happy with your body and how you look. From that point onwards, you might find yourself either falling into old bad eating patterns *or* falling into the extreme of undereating, over exercising, and being overly conscious of everything you put in your mouth.

As mentioned before, you should try to aim for balance, more than anything, and this includes your relationship with media frenzy as well. The images you see on your skin have little to do with the actual people behind them; they are a construct meant to make people feel like absolute perfection can and should be achieved. Instead of delivering to these expectations, however, the media regularly falls behind on its promises and ends up selling products and programs that are nothing but new variations of old tricks.

Again, this is not to say you should turn off your TV and disappear off the face of the internet. This is just to say that you should take the world behind the screens at its true value: fantasy and make-believe, not reality.

That being said, you should learn how to feel good in your own body regardless of where in your weight loss journey you might be. We will discuss mindset problems in the following section, but since this is very often related to how media portrayals of beauty have altered our perception of it, we thought it would be important to mention this here as well.

Yes, you can strive for better, but before you aim to look like Jennifer Lopez, remember that looking great is part of her job. Plus, she doesn't have a nine to five job she has to work, and there is a group of people paid to help her shine. The same goes for male role models as well, by the way.

The good part about the media is that it has started to change. You see more and more plus size models, fitness models, and, in general, models that do not fit the "traditional" stereotype. You see more role models advocating for health, as opposed to smaller clothing sizes. You see more and more celebrities who are open about the "fakeness" of their projections. Overall, you also see more and more acceptance as well.

The media and weight loss have been connected ever since the beginning of the dietary products industry. From newspaper ads that take up a lot of pages to Facebook ads and Instagram influencers, the diet industry has adapted to the novelty of these times. Given the changes we have seen in the last decade or so, there is a pretty high chance that the diet industry of 2030 will be completely different than the diet industry of the 1990s, and that can only be great news, really.

The Wrong Mindset

No matter your goals, you should always make sure you start on the right foot. If you want to learn how to paint, you have to start by thinking you can do this. If you want to learn how to cook, you have to start by thinking you can do this.

With weight loss, things can be a little more complicated. This is mostly due to the complexity of the mindset that leads to weight gain and the intricacy of the mindset that makes people *stay* in that area as well.

If you want to lose weight, however, it is essential to start on the right foot. More specifically, you should start with the right mindset. Some of the most important tips to keep in mind here include the following:

- **Stop calling it a "diet."** If you want your weight loss to actually function (and if you want to *keep* that weight off), you have to step out of the "diet" mindset. When dieting, people eat (or don't eat) certain things until they reach a certain weight goal and then revert to their old patterns. Instead of doing that, you should aim to change your entire lifestyle and be more balanced from a general point of view. The minute you call it a diet is the minute you have set the foundation of your mindset.
- **Don't think of failure.** We know it can be hard to do, especially after reading everything in this book so far, but trust us: weight loss is far from being impossible. It's just that it has been misrepresented and misunderstood. Don't even think of failure; just picture yourself at your goal weight.

- **Accept who you are right now.** If you start from a point of hatred and dismay towards your body, you cannot maintain a positive mindset across the entire process. Accept your beauty and attractiveness as you are right now and look at the weight loss process as a means by which you are refining yourself and aiming for the very best version of who you are and who you can be.
- **Don't think of weight loss as a painful process.** Indeed, changing your lifestyle and listening to your body can take time and practice, and it might not be the most pleasant thing ever. If you look at the bright side, though, you will realize that this whole process is wonderful and that you are heading towards something that is simply *better* for you and for your body.
- **Practicing Yoga and other meditation and mindfulness practices can actually help.** These practices will allow you to get more in tune with your body, to reconnect it with the mind, and to reach your goal weight as your *body* dictates, as opposed to as what anyone else might dictate.

Your mindset can really make or break your weight loss efforts, so set yourself in the right mental place and allow everything to stem from there. The more positive you are, the more satisfied you will be with the small victories, and the happier you will be with the big victories as well.

Changing your entire mindset in relation to food can be tough, and it does take determination. However, it is an essential element in your weight loss process, and it can really make a difference in the world. As you will see in the next chapter, you shouldn't have to change who you are and what you like to lose weight. Instead, you should just change the way in which you perceive your body and your food intake, as well as how you listen to the hunger and satiation cues your body is sending you.

Yes, you can definitely do this, and as surprising and unrealistic as it may seem, it all starts with good thoughts.

The Biggest Mistakes

Before we delve into the theory and tips behind intuitive eating, we would like to make a brief summary of everything we have discussed thus far. The first two chapters have been dedicated to teaching you the importance of knowing yourself and the causes that may have made people fail in their attempts to lose weight (once and for all).

The last section of these two chapters will be dedicated to summing up all the big mistakes people make when dieting (all of which are based on everything we have discussed thus far).

We don't want to keep you here for too long, much so knowing that you are probably quite curious to learn more about intuitive eating and everything it entails. As such, we will keep this section as short as possible. Keep in mind though: this is the foundation of intuitive eating, so we strongly recommend you take matters seriously.

So, what are, in short, the worst mistakes about dieting (and the reasons it so frequently fails to live up to one's expectations)?

The Idea of Dieting In Itself

Have you ever noticed how diets are always associated with a consistent negative feeling? It's almost as if "diet" is just "die" with a "t" added at the end. When someone turns down a slice of cake and says they're on a diet, it almost sounds as if the saddest thing in the world has just happened to them.

And in many ways, it has.

As we were saying before, food is not just a matter of nutrition. Food is actually good. It brings people together at dinner parties and helps us bond with each other on a first date. It's comforting and dopamine-inducing. It's more than just a way to stay alive in a biological sense; it is a way to stay alive in the philosophical meaning of the word.

Dieting has gotten a bad rep, and if we have to be completely honest, it's easy to see why. When "dieting" equals taking away everything you like to eat, it feels like simply taking away a slice from the cake called "joy of living."

The idea of dieting will put you in a bad mood from the very beginning of your weight loss process, and it will set you up for failure precisely because it is associated with negative feelings. Ditch the "diet" concept and allow yourself to live happily *and* healthily by simply listening to your body!

If you have never dieted before or if you have attempted to diet and failed, start by simply ditching the very concept of "dieting." It can really do wonders.

Not Understanding Your Body

Your body needs food to survive, and it definitely needs a little from all the macronutrients: carbohydrates/sugars, proteins, and fats. Each and every single one of these has an important role in your body, and you should not deprive it from getting what it needs just because you're on a "diet."

The reason most diets fail is because they are insufferably restrictive about certain food groups. Your body works *against* this precisely because it knows it needs more than what you are offering to it when you are dieting.

Understanding your body and what it needs is crucial in any weight loss (or conscious weight gain) effort. Read and learn about your body. But most importantly, learn how to get in touch with its wants and needs again. It is the single most important thing you should do to ensure the success of your weight loss process.

Not Understanding Your Mind

One of the most common reasons people overeat and binge is not because of their tummy, as much as it is their mind. When you understand your brain and your emotions, and when you learn to control them, you are less likely to overeat. This, together with our next point in this list will help you eliminate the two most important factors that push people into eating too much.

Understand your mental state so that you can understand your eating habits. If you have never dieted before, this will be one of the most important first steps towards weight loss. If you *have* dieted, you have probably already learned it the hard way; not trying to understand your mind and your body are among the biggest enemies of weight loss.

Not Understanding Food Intake

You don't have to be a nutritionist, and you don't have to measure calories for each and every single bite of food you put in your body to learn about food intake.

Yes, it does help to keep track of your caloric intake, but not because you should fall into a calorie counting obsession. The reason you should understand caloric intake is because it will help you figure out how much food is really enough.

In time, you won't need to count calories anymore, precisely because you will align your body and your mind to their true needs and as such, you will be able to just happily go about your new lifestyle.

Living for the Mass-Media

As we have emphasized in previous sections, mass media has been feeding us all with a lot of lies. Not all of mass media is bad, and as we have also mentioned before, change is on the horizon in terms of how we perceive weight loss and weight gain.

However, if you live for the mass media, if you want to lose weight because your favorite celebrities look a certain way, and if you wholeheartedly believe that everything on TV and on Instagram is 100% real, then you should revert your mindset.

No, those marvelous appearances are not 100% real. They are manufactured to mimic a generalized idea of "perfection." No, you shouldn't lose weight because celebrities are skinny. You should lose weight because it's the best thing you can do for your mind and your body. No, you shouldn't live for mass media and its standards. You should live for yourself and on your own rules.

Of course, there are many other mistakes people make when they try to lose weight. Regardless of whether you have tried it before or if this is your first time, one thing is for certain: the mistakes we have explained in this section are central to "diet failures" and they should be avoided at all costs.

It's high time we left behind unrealistic standards and expectations and started to truly understand our bodies, our minds, and our relationship with food. THIS is where a healthy lifestyle begins!

Chapter 3: Intuitive Eating — The No-Diet Diet

You might be brand new to the world of dieting (case in which our book is the ideal way to start) or you might have adventured into the weight loss realm before. Wherever you stand, you have come to the right place because so far, we've only shown you why most diets don't work.

As we have discussed before, there is something inherently wrong about dieting in a traditional point of view. The very fact that it starts like a chore and like the saddest thing in the world should be a red flag for pretty much anyone attempting to lose weight. How can anything be good for you if every single inch of your body and your mind are actively fighting against it?

The fact that we have been sold into marketing gimmicks by the weight loss industry doesn't help either. As shown earlier in the book, the vast majority of the so-called "diets" out there are either blatant lies or simply twisting old concepts (such as removing an entire group of food from one's menu).

As also shown earlier in the book, it's quite clear that statistics are very straightforward about dieting: nearly all diets fail, sooner or later. If you have never tried one before, the fact that you are here, reading this book, is only good news.

Intuitive eating is one of the best ways to lose weight, precisely because it taps into your body's natural tendencies. There's a good reason they call it *intuitive*: it actually is. In essence, intuitive eating is about following your body's cues and learning how to communicate with your body in an efficient and healthy way.

Believe it or not, we're all born capable of doing this. Take babies, for example. They will not scream or cry without any kind of reason. They will do it only when they are hungry, uncomfortable, or in need of care and attention. They naturally follow their bodies' cues of hunger and discomfort and know how to get what they need, when they need it.

Obviously, we are not advocating throwing tantrums whenever you need something. What we *are* advocating, however, is knowing how to listen to your body. All those diets out there are failing because they miss out on the one ingredient that matters: the "dieter" themselves.

You cannot take yourself out of the scheme and you cannot blindly follow the advice given by one fitness guru to another. Their tips might work, sure, but it is impossible to assume that they will work on *everyone*. And the reason this is true is because we're all different. What works for you might not work for your sister or neighbor, but it might work for someone on the opposite end of the globe, whom you've never met.

That being said, the best "guru" to follow is, well, none other than *yourself*. You should be the one who sets the rules when it comes to your weight loss program. This is the only way you can sustain the entire weight loss process throughout a long period of time (and make sure lost pounds stay off).

That being said, we will dedicate this chapter to teaching you about the basics behind intuitive eating and everything it means. We promise: it is the one *no diet* that actually works, precisely because it taps into YOUR needs and YOUR lifestyle.

45

What Is Intuitive Eating

In short, intuitive eating is a no-diet approach to weight loss and health that focuses on allowing yourself to truly listen to your body. It's an idea we have iterated and reiterated throughout the entire book, but this time we're expanding on it so that you can truly understand the concept behind it.

Intuitive eating is nothing new. In fact, it's been around for nearly a quarter of a century! Born in 1995, intuitive eating was developed as a response to the fad diet-infused world of the 1990s. If you think the world is going on crazy diets today, imagine that the 1990s were even more of a chaos in the weight loss realm.

As such, intuitive eating was developed by Evelyn Tribole and Elyse Resch, two dietitians who noticed that there was a lot of craze created around diets that not only failed to be sustainable in the long run, but frequently led to more weight gain as well.

Intuitive eating aims to reconnect the body and the mind and make them work together in harmony. You might be surprised to hear this but living the modern life has pushed our bodies and our minds farther and farther from each other. Reconnecting them is not even just about weight loss. It is about feeling good at a general level. It is about allowing yourself to *breathe* better, to *live* better, to *be happier*.

The science of intuitive eating relies on everything that's wrong in the world of dieting:

- The fact that most diets are not sustainable in the long run.

- The fact that most diets make false promises.
- The fact that most diets fail sooner or later.
- The fact that most diets feel like atrocious actions against the willingness of our own bodies.

Intuitive eating is meant to free you from misery: the misery of feeling guilty for what you eat, the misery of attempting to lose weight and knowing for a fact that there's a 95% chance you will not make it to your goal, the misery of not having a slice of cake on your birthday, and so on.

Intuitive eating is all about allowing yourself to be free and happy. About allowing yourself to be mindful of what you eat without feeling any kind of pressure and without restricting yourself from certain foods because they are deemed as "bad" or without feeling like your world will crumble if you have a burger.

It sounds ridiculous, but those of you who have been on a diet before can definitely attest to the fact that dieting is associated with a permanent state of misery, restriction, and sadness.

Weight loss doesn't have to be that way, though. It really doesn't have to feel like torment against every inch of your body and mind. It doesn't have to make you want to crawl back into bed and cry because you simply want to eat a slice of pizza.

This is not to say intuitive eating promotes unhealthy eating habits or fast foods; it's just to say that intuitive eating promotes balance. More than anything, intuitive eating is about being aware of your body's needs, of what you truly need to eat, and ultimately, about being happy with who you are, where you are, and what you are eating,

Intuitive eating is not:

- **A diet.** By definition, a diet involves restrictions of some sort. Some diets focus on restricting certain types of foods. Others focus on restricting calorie intake. Others focus on restricting when you can eat. Intuitive eating restricts nothing. It just focuses on allowing your body and your mind to correctly communicate their needs in relation to food.
- **Mindful eating.** Although mindfulness will definitely help when it comes to intuitive eating, there is a clear difference to be made between "mindful" eating and "intuitive" eating. The difference lies in the fact that mindful eating is all about focusing on the act of eating itself (how you chew, the taste of your food, the kind of nutrients that go into your body, and even the source of those nutrients). These practices can help when it comes to intuitive eating, but they are not the main focus of intuitive eating.
- **A magic promise.** Intuitive eating restricts nothing, but that doesn't mean you can just binge eat fast food and drink loads of sugary drinks every day. Yes, you can allow yourself the occasional "slip," but be very attentive to the signals your body is sending you when you eat so-called "bad" foods, especially when it happens for prolonged periods of time. Do you really feel *good* about it? Does your body feel energized and happy once you finish eating or does it feel quite the opposite?

Intuitive eating is not a meal plan, nor is it a diet that will promise you to lose X amount of pounds in Y number of months. Intuitive eating allows you to take your own course, to follow your own cues, to set your own rules. The key is making sure that you genuinely listen to your body and what it needs, to the things that make it feel good and the things that make it feel not that great.

The dieting culture has taught us to settle for less and for tasteless foods that do not provide us with pleasure. But things don't have to be this way, and the best example we can give here is the French culture.

Although the French eat quite a lot of pastry and cheese and they won't even imagine a meal without a glass of wine, the rate of obesity is considered to be one of the lowest in the OECD (Fryar, Carroll & Ogden, 2016). Although obesity rates have been steadily increasing in France as well (most likely due to the dieting culture more than anything), the country is still quite far away from the rates of obesity in the United States. To be more specific, in 2014, about 24% of the French people were considered to be obese (with a BMI of 30 or more), while in the same year, in the USA, nearly 38% of the adults were considered to be obese (OECD, n.d.).

The key is knowing when to eat, what to eat, how much to eat, and there's no rule book to dictate what your own body perceives as good, bad, or enough. Yes, you should definitely listen to the American Heart Association. And yes, you should definitely try to get more of those greens and veggies into your body.

Yet, at the end of the day, guilt trips down the darkness of your kitchen at midnight will do nothing good for you—physically or mentally. The very fact that you are guilty about having a slice of cheese or a cup of whole milk makes it extremely easy to fall into a pattern of guilt, remorse, false reward, and misery.

Why Is It a Solution?

If this is the first time you try to lose weight, intuitive eating is the best way to do it precisely because it will keep you away from the cycle of misery we mentioned before. Even more, intuitive eating is a mild, natural, and caring way to lose weight. Instead of forcing yourself into restrictions, you will simply allow your body to proceed on a more natural path for it.

If you have tried dieting before but haven't succeeded, you will also find that intuitive eating is a much better solution than whatever type of diet you may have tried before. We will discuss a bit about this in the section at hand, but overall, intuitive eating will pretty much "fix" whatever didn't go well with previous diets you may have dabbled in.

Intuitive eating is a solution because it goes against everything wrong with the diet industry as a whole:

- It is not a diet in the traditional sense of the word because, as mentioned before it does not restrict anything.
- It does not sell false dreams,
- It does not push you against your own body.
- It does not make you feel miserable about eating something you like.
- It does not restrict you from things you love eating.
- It allows your mind and your body to fully reconnect.
- It helps you lose weight in a natural, steady, and sustainable way.
- It can be "followed" for the rest of your life.
- It does not attempt to make you buy any kind of "magic product."

Statistically, intuitive eating truly is the best choice, both for those who have dieted before and for those who want to lose weight for the first time in their lives. Numerous studies show that intuitive eating is not only effective from a weight-related point of view, but also from the point of view of one's self-esteem and positive body image (Studies, n.d.).

In addition to the fact that intuitive eating is great for people who want to lose weight and simply feel better in their own skin, it is also quite important to mention that intuitive eating has been proven efficient in the case of those who suffer from certain eating disorders as well.

Intuitive eating is a solution because it doesn't force you into anything. It allows you to be free, and ultimately, allows you to be genuinely happy with who you are and what you are doing for your health and general well-being.

Intuitive eating works precisely because it goes against everything that doesn't work. It is a solution to a world that has gone mad over dieting and, in the process, has forgotten the basics:

- Your body actually knows what to do and what it needs.
- Your mind is strongly connected to your body.
- Food should still be a pleasure, regardless of whether or not you are "dieting."

Intuitive eating is worth a go because it will allow you to get in touch with your true self and with your real needs. Once you listen to your body and once you know what triggers you to go against your body's natural needs (e.g. by binge eating), everything else will fall into place.

How Do You Practice Intuitive Eating?

Intuitive eating is based on 10 crucial principles, which we will discuss in the last section of this book. In addition to this, we also want to emphasize the importance of avoiding overeating, as this is one of the most common reasons people cannot truly listen to the needs of their bodies when it comes to food.

As such, this last section of our book will be split into two main parts: the rules of intuitive eating and tips on how to avoid overeating and binge eating.

The 10 Principles of Intuitive Eating

1. Forgo the Concept of Dieting

This is something we have emphasized from the very introduction of this book, and it is also the first (and probably one of the foremost important) principles of intuitive eating as well.

The diet mentality has been proven to do nothing good for anyone. It makes people feel miserable, it makes people miss out on one of the biggest joys of life, and in the end, it is inefficient by definition.

Don't put yourself on a diet. Put yourself on a lifestyle change you can support in the long run and truly adhere to for the decades to come.

2. Eat When Hungry

Nobody can tell you how many meals you should eat in a day. Some people need one meal and a couple of snacks, other people need several meals. That's OK.

The key is making sure you eat when you are hungry, rather than eat when you are told to. We have been taught to follow a three main course-meal pattern since childhood, but the truth is that it might not work for everyone.

Know when you are hungry and honor your feelings. When you start eating when you are hungry instead of "when you are supposed to," you are also far less likely to end up in a binge session at the end of the day.

3. Be at Peace with Food

Let's make this clear once and for all: food is not your enemy. Food nourishes your body with the nutrients it needs to keep on going. Even more, food nourishes your mind by providing you with little moments of pleasure, which, by the way, you should learn to enjoy to the fullest.

There is a reason all major celebrations in one's life involve food: eating together is an act that bonds people (and it has been doing that from the very beginnings of Homo Sapiens). Honor that and make peace with food by enjoying its beauty, taste, and its value for your body.

4. There's No "Bad" Food

There are foods that might be better for your body than others, true. Whole foods, lean meats, complex carbs, fruit and vegetables—they are universally known to be healthy for one's body.

Beyond all that, however, no food is inherently bad. You can still have an occasional burger or slice of cake if it brings you pleasure, and you can still enjoy meals out with your friends.

The key lies in making sure you do not exaggerate. If you listen to your body, it will automatically know when you have been having too much of a food that does not provide you with nutritional value. Listen and follow your body's signals.

5. Reconnect with the Pleasure of Eating

The Japanese see healthy living in ways that are entirely different from everything we have known in the Western culture. The very fact that they include the *pleasure of eating* in their concept of a healthy lifestyle makes a world of a difference from every point of view.

Reconnecting with the pleasure of eating will allow you to be actually more balanced about it. When you enjoy the occasional treats, you are feeding your mind and your body with something it truly enjoys, something that brings you happiness. This doesn't mean you should go over the top and only eat cake or pizza every day. It just means that you should savor the moments of indulgence and take them as such. It means that you should not feel guilty for allowing yourself brief moments of "sin."

It also means that eating should actually satisfy your body's nutritional needs as much as it should satisfy your taste buds. Believe it or not, "healthy food" does not have to equal "tasteless food," and there are thousands of ways in which you can rediscover the value in ingredients that are both healthy and delicious.

6. Know When You Are Full

As we were saying earlier in the book, you could (theoretically) gain weight from eating nothing but kale leaves. Everything in excess will lead to weight gain, and not even the healthiest foods in the world are an exception from this rule.

You do not have to count calories or Weight Watcher points to know when you are full. You just have to eat slowly, focus on your actual act of eating, and listen to when your body says you have had enough.

It takes a bit of practice to learn how to do this, but once you get it, you will never feel the need to overeat, not even with the most delicious foods you love so much.

7. Show Yourself Some Kindness

The dieting culture has been putting us all on a lot of pressure. Looking perfect has somewhat become the ultimate goal in life for so many, and in the case for this perfection, too many have lost themselves.

Show yourself kindness. Your mind and your body are supporting you every day of your life. They are your armor against the tumultuous waves of the world. They allow you to exist in the fullest sense of the word. They allow you to laugh, to share memories with your loved ones, or to simply enjoy the purr of a kitten.

Be kind with yourself and your body. The kinder you are, the more likely it is that you will be in full touch with everything surrounding you. More importantly, you will be more in touch with *yourself* and that's the most solid foundation you can build for intuitive eating and a healthy lifestyle that can be supported in the long run.

8. Respect Yourself and Your Body

There are thousands of ways in which you can respect your body. The fact that you dress in nice clothes is just the surface. The fact that you consciously choose to feed yourself with foods that are fully nutritious and healthy is one of the deepest acts of respect you can do for your body.

Respect who you are and where you come from. Respect your journey, the food you put in your body and its sources, every inch of skin on your body and every muscle that makes you laugh every day.

It's an act of compassion and kindness, more than anything. An act that will help you make mindful and conscious choices about the foods you put in your body.

9. Feed Yourself with Nutritious Foods

No, there are no bad foods. Carbs are not evil, and not even that slice of chocolate cake can be inherently *bad* for you as long as you don't have it every day.

Feed your body with respect and care, with foods that give it what it truly needs: proteins for the muscles and for movement, carbohydrates for energy, and fats for good functioning of the brain and the entire system that supports your body.

Feed yourself with foods that are as whole and as unprocessed as possible. The more of these you put in your body, the more thankful it will be towards you.

10.   Move as Much as You Can

Exercise is not just an action you should mindlessly engage in every evening at the gym. It is an act of kindness and respect towards your body. It is an action that allows you to stay healthy at a physical and mental level. It is an act you are doing for yourself first and foremost.

As we were also saying towards the beginning of this book, exercising does not have to mean "weightlifting." It can be anything else you enjoy like yoga, dancing, or just brisk walking, if that makes you happy.

As long as you keep your heart pumping and your body moving, the "best type of exercise" is that which makes you feel good about yourself.

Factors that Lead to Overeating

Following the 10 Principles of Intuitive Eating is essential. On top of that, however, you should also understand the reasons that lead to overeating and how to manage them. We have already discussed how to avoid binge eating, but we will retouch on the subject in a bit more detail here, precisely because it is such a crucial one (and not just when it comes to intuitive eating).

In general, the main factors that lead to overeating are the following:

- **The people you hang out with.** We are not saying in any kind of way that you should ditch your friends. What we are saying is that you should be more mindful of their choices and avoid being tempted by them. Yes, they might have made unhealthy choices for themselves but that doesn't mean you have to follow in their pattern as well. Try to avoid overeating when going out by simply practicing the same 10 Principles of Intuitive Eating mentioned in the previous section. This will allow you to stay away from temptation and eat only as much as you need to.

- **Not drinking enough water.** You might find this surprising, but many times, the brain cannot make the difference between a feeling of hunger and a feeling of thirst. Provide your body with the hydration it needs and allow yourself to listen to the difference between hunger and thirst!

- **Your plates are too big.** We have been taught to eat everything on our plate, but the truth is that this may not always be to our advantage especially when the plate is both too large and too full. Learn to know when you are feeling satiated based on your body's signals, rather than whether or not the plate is empty.

- **You are tired.** People who don't sleep enough are prone to overeating and developing slows your metabolism. Yes, you have a lot of work to do and yes, you might want to watch another episode of that new show on Netflix. But your sleep is much more important than all of this, so get plenty of it and allow your body to regenerate every night!

- **You are bored.** Let's face it: how many times have you found yourself mindlessly munching on snacks just because you were bored? Learn to channel your energies elsewhere (such as in a hobby, for example) and avoid boredom-eating. This can truly make a difference!

- **You've had too much alcohol.** You shouldn't deny yourself the occasional glass of wine, but keep in mind that too much alcohol can make you hungry. Make sure you know your limits when it comes to drinking, and make sure you don't go overboard because it will have a series of unpleasant effects on your body and on your mental state.
- **Eating too quickly.** Take your time when eating. You might think you're doing yourself a favor by rushing through your lunch before you get back to work, but the truth is that you are not. You won't spend more than five extra minutes if you take the time to correctly chew your food, but the benefits of doing it are tremendous!
- **The "diet mentality."** If you have ever dieted, and if you have fallen off the wagon, you might have found yourself disappointed and ready to repeat the same "mistake" precisely because you have relapsed in a sense in the first place. The diet mentality will only make you end up in a never-ending cycle of sin and guilt that will affect your weight, your self-confidence, and your ability to ever trust "diets" again.

"I have already ruined the diet," "I will start on Monday," and "I really feel deprived of good food" are the three most common thoughts that lead to overeating, and the underlying reasons people fail to stick to their diets as well.

When you free yourself from the diet mentality and allow yourself occasional indulgences without feeling like you have made a major mistake, you are less likely to overeat. You will go about your little pleasure as you would normally do it and then revert to living a healthy life as you have planned to do it.

Intuitive eating is, well, intuitive. It comes natural and it definitely follows your body's natural tendencies. All you need to do is reconnect to your body and truly listen to what it has to say about your dietary choices. Yoga and mindfulness practices can definitely help with this, as they will allow you to think in a way that takes your entire being into consideration. Yet, if you are not particularly keen on practicing Yoga or Tai-Chi, pretty much any act of relaxation will help.

A long bubble bath with candles and music, reading a good book, or planting flowers in your garden are actions that allow you to run from the stress of the mundane and communicate with your own self, with your body, and with your mind. They are also actions that show you are kind and compassionate with your own self, so practice them as much as you can. They may not have a direct influence on your weight loss process, but they can definitely help you stay on top of things.

Practice intuitive eating as if it's not a diet, but like a set of guidelines that allow you to free yourself from the mediatic lies and marketing approaches and tap into your true needs. Your body will follow in. It will shed the extra pounds up to a point that is healthy for you, and it will support you for the many decades to come.

Honor yourself, your mind, and your body. It is the one way to live happily, healthily, and far from the madding crowd of the diet world!

Conclusion

If you even attempt to Google "how to lose weight," you might find yourself bombarded with a treasure trove of information. We clearly have access to a lot more information than our mothers and fathers did back in the day, but together with the free spread of tips and tricks by pretty much everyone, we have also witnessed the fall of *valuable, accurate,* and *truthful* information as well.

The world of Pinterest, Instagram, and Facebook have done nothing else than emphasize a problem that has been building up for over a century: people are insecure about their bodies and companies are ready to take profit from this.

The absolute truth about everything you see on Instagram, Pinterest, and Facebook is that *pretty much 90% of it is fake.* People are consistently projecting images that are not only unrealistic, but they are also projecting entire lives that are far from everything real.

Yes, life through an Insta filter may seem a bit pinker, but when you come back from cloud nine and touch ground again, you will realize that nobody around you lives an actually Insta-worthy life.

So, why then would you ever believe in tips and tricks offered by people who cannot even put up with their own natural eye color on Instagram? Why would you believe in Paleo, Keto, or Lemon Juice diets, when it is quite clear that the very people promoting them are not *actually* following them either?

The issue of false diets and magic pills is not new, obviously. Before the internet, there were magazines, newspapers, posters, and TV channels that advertised the same kind of things. The issue with the "democratization" of information over the internet is that these days, these tips are not even offered by celebrities, but by people who are "average" in appearance and whose opinion you would have listened to back in the day.

What only a handful of these influencers tell you is that they are heavily editing all of their content and that they are being paid serious money by companies to sell you things you do not need and diet products that will eventually fail to live up to the hype.

What, then?

Whom should you believe?

Who is the true "guru" of the diet world now at the beginning of the third decade of the third millennium?

In reality, the only one you should ever listen to is your own body, and this book has explained *why* in as much detail as possible. In a world that is ramping out of control when it comes to dieting and "perfect" images, the only one you can truly trust is, well, your own body. Believe it or not, we have been engineered to actually know what we need, how much is enough, and where our healthy weight lies—we don't need diet pills, restrictions, and intricate spreadsheets to figure it all out.

Intuitive eating is all about reconnecting your mind and your body and bringing them together to work for your own advantage. It might seem like a "crazy" and unrealistic approach to weight loss, but the absolute truth is that it is the only method that can show actual results for the long run.

Diets fail because they cannot be customized to your own needs, to what you like, or to your own life. Diets fail because they make people feel miserable when they fall off the wagon *and* when they don't. Diets fail because they feel unnatural and forced.

Intuitive eating does none of these things. It follows your own signals, your own rules, and your own wishes of freedom. It allows you to breathe in a world of stringent dieters who advocate the second-coming of corsets from a philosophical point of view. It allows you to move at your own pace in a world that has forgotten to truly enjoy the happiness of food, of sharing food, and allowing food to fully touch your body in a healthy and positive way.

Intuitive eating is all about being positive, being yourself, and allowing yourself to exist against the crazy trends out there. It is about accepting yourself, loving yourself, and respecting yourself at the same time.

It is about breaking the mold, the stereotypes, the food-shaming and the fat-shaming.

It is about being free as a bird and living your best life, in your best body.

Nobody can dictate what you do with your own body. Nobody can tell you carbs are inherently evil when you feel miserably hungry without them. Nobody can tell you that you are not allowed a slice of your own birthday cake. And nobody can tell you that you should feel ashamed in any way, shape, or form.

Intuitive eating is, more than anything, about loving every inch of your body and allowing it to truly connect you with your future self, your best self, your healthiest needs and wants.

Intuitive eating is about YOU and how YOU choose to live your life to the fullest!

References

AHA. (n.d.). American Heart Association Recommendations for Physical Activity in Adults and Kids. Retrieved from https://www.heart.org/en/healthy-living/fitness/fitness-basics/aha-recs-for-physical-activity-in-adults

ANAD. (n.d.). Eating Disorder Statistics National Association of Anorexia Nervosa and Associated Disorders. Retrieved from https://anad.org/education-and-awareness/about-eating-disorders/eating-disorders-statistics/

Dray, Tammy. (n.d.). Facts & Statistics About Dieting. Retrieved from https://www.livestrong.com/article/390541-facts-statistics-about-dieting/

Economic Costs of Obesity. (n.d.). Retrieved from https://www.healthycommunitieshealthyfuture.org/learn-the-facts/economic-costs-of-obesity/

Fryar, C., Carroll, M., & Ogden, C. (2016). Prevalence of Overweight, Obesity, and Extreme Obesity Among Adults Aged 20 and Over: United States, 1960–1962 Through 2013–2014. Retrieved from https://www.cdc.gov/nchs/data/hestat/obesity_adult_13_14/obesity_adult_13_14.htm

Gunners, K. (2017). 12 Popular Weight Loss Pills and Supplements Reviewed. Retrieved from https://www.healthline.com/nutrition/12-weight-loss-pills-reviewed

Krisch, J. (2016). How Evolution Is Making Our Wisdom Teeth Disappear. Retrieved from https://www.vocativ.com/301772/evolution-wisdom-teeth/index.html

Mcleod, S. (2018). Maslow's Hierarchy of Needs. Retrieved from https://www.simplypsychology.org/maslow.html

Miller, K. (2015). Study: Most Children Start Dieting at Age 8. Retrieved from https://www.refinery29.com/en-us/2015/01/81288/children-dieting-body-image

OECD. (n.d.). Obesity and the Economics of Prevention: Fit not Fat - France Key Facts. Retrieved from https://www.oecd.org/els/health-systems/obesityandtheeconomicsofpreventionfitnotfat-francekeyfacts.htm

Sanyal, D., & Raychaudhuri, M. (2016). Hypothyroidism and obesity: An intriguing link. *Indian Journal of Endocrinology and Metabolism, 20*(4), 554-557.

Shahbandeh, M. (2019). U.S Diets and Weight Loss - Statistics & Facts. Retrieved from https://www.statista.com/topics/4392/diets-and-weight-loss-in-the-us/

Studies. (n.d.). Retrieved from https://www.intuitiveeating.org/resources/studies/

Watson, S. (2020). Blood Type Diet: Eating for Types O, A, B, & AB. Retrieved from https://www.webmd.com/diet/a-z/blood-type-diet

Weiss, Christine. (n.d.). Statistics on Dieting and Eating Disorders. Retrieved from https://www.montenido.com/pdf/montenido_statistics.pdf

WHO. (2020). Obesity and Overweight. Retrieved from https://www.who.int/news-room/fact-sheets/detail/obesity-and-overweight

Printed in Great Britain
by Amazon